Off the Beaten Path

Poems

by

Gary Lechliter

Off the Beaten Path

Copyright © 2014 by Gary Lechliter

All rights reserved

Woodley Press
Washburn University
Topeka, Kansas

ISBN: 978-0-9854586-9-0

Edited by: Kevin Rabas

Cover image by Dave Leiker
Dave Leiker Photography
http://prairiedust.zenfolio.com

kudos to Cheryl Unruh
http://www.flyoverpeople.net

Cover design: Pam LeRow

Book design: Pam LeRow

Published in the United States of America

Printed by Lightning Source Inc. (US)

for Thomas Zvi Wilson

Table of Contents

I

Jenny Wren 3
Solitude 4
Even Sock Monkeys Get the Blues 5
The Water Is Smoky with Mud 6
Milk and Lemon 7
Nocturne for Mrs. McMahon 8
The Woman Next-door 9
Incident at Riders Ford 10
Meanwhile 11
My Father's Daughter 12
Sunday Morning 13
Sidetracked 14
So Here We Are 15
Ghost Roses 16
Camping in the Stull Cemetery 17
Girl 18
Ghost Town 19
I Saw You at the Bait Shop 20
The Wind Dancing Across the Prairie 21
Halloween 22
Winter and Other Illusions 23
The Night Bus 24
At the Present 26
Things Happen in Threes 27
I Have Decided 28
Off the Beaten Path 29

II

The Night It Rained for Years 33
OZ Revisited 34
Dog Logic 35
Taking the Dog Out 36
Tree in a Field 37
You Might Wake Up 38
Whoever You Are 39
Clearing 41

Days of Work and Reason 42
For James Wright 43
Late in the Day 44
The Ghost of My Father's Ghost 45
What I Know About Ghosts 46
Open Range 47
Phew! 48
Pondering 49
To Simply Live 50
Hoarfrost 51
The Year of the Gadfly 52
Bluestem 53
The Bishop's Wife Revisited 54
The Boy Who Kissed His Sister 55
The Fiddler 56

III

Boy 59
Rooster 60
The Porpoise Drive-In Life 62
Hay Barn 63
She Had Horses 64
Nothing to Do with Horses 65
The Gospel of Bubba 66
She Sings Pink Floyd 68
Once in a Meadow 69
Horsefeathers 70
Bonfire of the Sleepless Poet 71
In Case of Aging 72
Bird Flu Gloves 73
The Night We Heard the Whippoorwill 74
Awakened by Silence 75
Shades of Gray 76
The Ivory-billed Woodpecker 77
The View from Sanders Mound 78
Vultures in a Dead Tree 79
Stranger at the Door 80
Curtain Call 81
While She Sleeps 82
Bile Diary 83
Vespers 84

Off the Beaten Path

I

Jenny Wren

The girl I loved for years
was diaphanous, hard to hold.
Late in the evening, especially
past midnight, she came to me,

no questions asked, slept snug
in my bed, as snow that drifted
from a hole in the wall dusted
the sheets, while we shivered
and shed our childhood skins.

Love came natural as snow.
Alone in the house we danced
close, and no one called her
to come home, she was free
as the ectoplasm that warmed

nothing, but kept things whole.
She had many faces and names:
Grace, Marilyn, Janis Joplin,
to me she was all the same.

I called her Diana Ross one
night, and she was Diana Ross.
I made love to Diana Ross!
I, a schmuck of a boy, with

no place to go, nothing to be,
made love to Diana Ross!
If I wanted the cheerleader
no boy could hold, she was
her in a moment's notice.

And sometimes Jenny Wren
winked and laughed in the
afterglow of sex, one cigarette
smoked in a hurry, leaving its
ash and tar on the sheets.

Solitude

My mother wanted light in the house,
especially in winter, when darkness
crept through the neighborhood.
She loved chandeliers with naked
bulbs, that raised her depression,
and held her firmly to faith.

But I hated the light that swarmed
our house. The light-bulbs with obscene
pounding drove me to seek tranquility
with cobwebs and winter ghosts.
I sat in the half-dark for hours and talked to
shades, agreeing with their prose.

I began to understand that faces I saw
in the dingy wallpaper were only visible
on the retinas of a troubled boy.
And no one would believe me if I told them
I saw the face of Reverend Showalter,
who once sicked Jesus on me.

Even Sock Monkeys Get the Blues

And why shouldn't they? Nobody
wants them to horribly squat on

their beds, button eyes that stare
into space, and do not find love.

You can't get a dime for one, even
if your sainted grandmother

made it with the hope you would
cherish the godforsaken thing

that slumps through the house at night,
dour, knuckle-walking, searching

for the secret graveyard, where they
lie in heaps, passé and torn.

The Water Is Smoky with Mud

(Translation from the Osage word for Neodesha, Kansas)

And I know the water,
the rocks and moss.
Downstream the bend
and adjacent riffles.
The smell of familiar
ash on the riprap.
Above the dam, farm-
fields and hedge.

The river is smoky
with mud and memory
of the girl who barely
knew me, said she
could never love me,
and nearly gave
herself on the cutbank,
but held onto Christ.

Faith's inhibition
nearly smoked, I held
her quietly, moved
with guilt, tossing to
the water the condom
I bought for 25 cents
from the vending machine
at Bob's Texaco.

The water, transient,
muddy and fogged,
swirled darkly past
knots of driftwood,
the knee-joints of old
trees, rooted and firm,
the girl in her soiled half-
slip, shuddering.

Milk and Lemon

We fell in love down by the
sea, near Coffeyville, Kansas,
where waves crash the prairie
and push toward Oklahoma.

All the mermaids in the sea of grass
sat pleasantly among the cows
that swarmed around and mewled.

As a beached jellyfish smiled
at her she called for butter and
bread, a tea cozy, milk and lemon.
And we went on with love's
idea, having nothing else to do.

Stolen bicycles emerged from
the waves, coughed through
their spokes racked with playing
cards that clattered in gyre.

We left the sea and wandered
old highways, gray and worn.
She said her life would spiral
in despair without the sea.

"We need the sea," she said,
as we hitchhiked with no destination.
No probable sea was evident
through the labyrinth of asphalt.

I don't remember, after all
the years have quickly blown,
what became of the lost girl,
whose touch could rescue all the
ships at sea in peril of loss.

Perhaps she wanders blithely
on the plains, along the ethereal
beach, singing *Peace Be Still*
to calm the lespedeza.

Nocturne for Mrs. McMahon

At night I escort myself
through a ghost town
where streets are battered
brick, chipped and ribbed,
like the place I once called home.
Sometimes I stop to look
around the neighborhood.

And it becomes apparent
that nothing dies like
a street, no one lives here
anymore; all the houses have
fallen, like dominos tipped.

Not even the Frisco Depot
remains, where as a boy I
snuck from my bedroom window
and stood transfixed by
the rise and fall of rails
as the night trains rattled by.

Tonight I hear the chorus
of those who went before me:
the engineers and coalmen,
farmers, grease monkeys,
the hired laundry woman,
hunched over the ironing board,
chain-smoking.

The Woman Next-door

was a preacher's kid, whose
husband was stationed in Vietnam.
Lonely, she searched for touch
if she could find it, momentary
sin to assuage the longing.
I was the boy next-door, sixteen,
awkward, thin as a bolt.

She invited me in to her house
to hear the 45 record she loved:
Poor Side of Town, by Johnny Rivers.
And who but a Baptist could not
dance slow and close to that song?
Shaky, I held her like one of the
school girls I nearly loved.

As we danced, I swear on Buddha's
head she pulled me to the couch
and whispered, "Just lie on top
like we're making love, but please
don't kiss me, or I won't be able
to stop until we've sinned in front
of God and the law."

As the record changed, Percy Sledge
crooned how a man loves a woman,
and we held tight in the venue
of passion bound by restraint.
Then she pushed me off, apologized,
smoothed her blouse, dabbed
her eyes and blew her nose.

Incident at Riders Ford

(Winter, 1967)

More feminine than girls I knew,
he had more verve than the boys.
Quiet and polite, he was easily bullied
by Baptists and Catholics alike.
All the bible-thumpers preached that
different people are doomed.

This is how it was in the Heartland,
for anyone far from the norm.
He wore panties beneath his slacks.
Someone said he was queer.
But the rumor was never vetted.

All that mattered in our town
was to fit in where you could, do your
part, walk like a man and spit snuff,
gaze through cracks in the girl's shower,
say fuck daily just to say it, damn
the Russians, the Chinese, the Jews.

But he would have none of bigotry.
A kind soul with a warm smile,
the FFA boys took him to the river,
depantsed him and left him naked
in darkness that hides stupidity.

When the police found him dazed
and shivering in the street,
he refused to identify the thugs
or press charges, and nothing
was done; they got away with
simian, primordial acts.

Meanwhile

There's a woman
with a knapsack
standing around
on the sidewalk.
Just standing there,
doing nothing
but shaking her
hair to let it fall,
and wipe the rain
from her glasses.
Meanwhile the rain
falls in the river,
the dark fast water
that flows past the
living and the dead:
the humpback drunk
and homeless bard
of muddled muse,
the junior g-man
with a third eye,
a boy who wears
his sister's bra
with Kleenex falsies,
tall and graceful
in high heel boots,
the glans confused by
inchoate breasts.

My Father's Daughter

My father's daughter,
who was stillborn in winter,
lives in a clapboard shack
by the coal-piles.

My father's daughter
knows there are never
available men in the town,
where she irons shirts

and sells tomatoes
from the hood of her
flatbed truck. And with
the moon half-hung,

half-full, she haunts
the fields at harvest time,
her hair blown dark,
tasseled like corn.

Sunday Morning

I am not walking down the street
whistling an ancient hymn.

Instead, I sit in the living room
beside the fireplace edged in soot.

Wrens haggle and cheep in the yews.
Boredom hangs from my face.

The neighbor's hound announces
that the wind is chasing a wild blouse.

A cat mewls from the long grass.
Somebody slams their car door.

Two hours later, drunk on
dullness, I rise to shake off the demons,

brush my teeth, pinch the knolls
on my hips, put some clean socks on.

Sidetracked

It's good to walk on the railroad
tracks, the sad rails, no longer used,
that seem at first glance to lead
nowhere, then take me by the
soul and scatter what I have learned
like dust to the wind.

I walk the old tracks, abandoned,
rusted, the crossties splintered,
left by railroads that went the way
of all things chosen for loss.

Prairie grasses wave at my passing.
Combines dust the air with husk.
Snakes wander across the chat.
Crows hunch on the power poles.

I pause to take a look around,
and find no one tied to the tracks,
no silent movie damsel to save
from the locomotive that no longer
rattles through a veil of soot
to the switchback.

So Here We Are

Maybe you're just sitting there
watching the day pass by, each
hour straying like lambs from the flock.

I'm at my desk, looking around
the room, listening to nothing
outside the window
drag its fingernail across the glass.

Then a duck waddles in, one of
those white, domestic birds,
smoking a cigar, drooling on the carpet,
wearing a blue house dress.

He too looks around the room,
his pink apron bearing the stains
of yesterday's egg and coffee.

Pinfeathers flutter to the floor.
As the room revolves around us
he hands me a shiny tract that will

surely save my soul, at the cost of
freedom of thought and difference.
I don't want to accept the pamphlet
that wreaks of the wrath of God.

And maybe you're just sitting there
with brain farts about to burst,
as the duck begins to witness.

Ghost Roses

In our days of adolescence,
when we wrestled on the
floor, it's true she laughed
when I pulled her pigtails,
and I could never pin her.

Then it seemed enough
to know the comfort
sisters give to rangy
boys without agenda
for living in Kansas.

It was good to have her
to hold in the tempest
that blew through our
house, my father in his
cups, mother hanging
on the best she could.

I cannot define her
more than the sister
who died at birth, when
wind harped in the trees.
Maybe she never lived
outside my skull,

and maybe my head
is a fine garden to haunt,
all the worm passages
that spiral through aging
lobes, where she walks
through the rose trellis
to pick the pink ones.

Camping in the Stull Cemetery

We join hands and form a circle,
letting the fire crack until blue.
Standing together in the timothy,
we burst suddenly into dance.
Intensely loving one another,
we roll in the weeds and pick
cocklebur from our backs.

We remember why we love.
And that becomes our coin.
Lying all night by dark woods,
framed in the moon's old slurry,
wrapped in the crazy quilt
of modern life, we drink the
good wine until it's gone.

No one sulks about the end
of the world, wars and rumors
of war, apocalyptic horsemen,
driverless cars, heads rolling free.
We've had enough of angst.
Lying close to the fire we hear
the June bugs pop.

Girl

You with the farm face
cannot know me as anything
more than man-shadow
seen darkly through the fog.
You, petite girl, wet-haired
and coatless in December
know that as our species behaves
you will not trust strangers
and passers by.

For I who mean you
the least harm of anyone
speeding on 40 west
might not be trustworthy
for all you know.
And you don't see me
or the faceless driver
in the next car that passes,
the next one after that.

Riders of the winter mist,
dazed and bemused by chill,
do not belong to any
organization for the needless
rescue of deer-eyed waifs
like you, girl, or the next girl
standing by the road,
waiting in different snow
for the same bus.

Ghost Town

Bars closed and jobs lost.
Train tracks, rusted, free

to run absolutely nowhere,
go nowhere and carry nothing with them

but diesel smoke blown
from the fiery bellies

of night-trains rattling past
gas pumps abandoned.

I Saw You at the Bait Shop

I saw you at the bait shop
weeping for innocent minnows,
stuffing night crawlers into your purse,
trying like hell to smuggle them
to the sanctuary for abused worms.
You stood there in your dungarees,
where crayfish clattered in buckets.

Nobody else saw you, shoplifter,
walk around with crickets in your bra
and shrimp in your panties.
This is not to say that you might
have been arrested, taken downtown,
fingerprinted, strip-searched
and thrown in the hoosegow.

It's just that I have a crush on you,
and only a fink would snitch.
So there we were, uncomfortable
moments passing, the shad-guts
you dumped on the floor in
a rage stewing in the heat
and stench.

The Wind Dancing Across the Prairie

(for my other self)

This sure as hell
ain't Texarkana,
I say to myself,
as the arctic blast

hits like the last
frozen ghost train
from Minneapolis.
O alter ego, my brain,

like a slide projector,
flicks back through dust
to a summer weekend
in Kansas City.

We rented Rocky Horror.
Both of us got drunk
and silly enough to mimic
the Time Warp song.

Thinking about it now
I am nearly frantic.
At this time of year
stress overthrows me.

The wind keeps doing
her slow striptease,
hoarfrost bump-grind
skin dance

of late snow squalls,
the death dance
for tulips
and frail magnolia.

Halloween

The youngest of the herd
arrive before the gloaming.
Some, carried by their mothers,
weep at the least little thing.
They have a long way to go in
the neighborhood, around the
block might seem a sojourn.

In darkness that intensifies
the autumn chill, here come the
older kids with more experience.
If we don't go to the door and
give the candy they will leave
disenchanted, and we'll hold
the badge of old grumps.

On the porch stands a local girl
dressed as Peter Pan, and her
brother who mimics Tinkerbelle.
The neighbor's son portrays an
ersatz Elvis. And Jerry Garcia,
looking well and praiseful,
strolls past in midair.

Winter and Other Illusions

Nothing looks right in February,
with green and blossom on-hold.
Trees moan in the night for loss,
and lost dogs roam the streets.

Banshees, naked and translucent,
howl in alleyways and fields.
Bowling alley parking lots glisten
with cars heaped in slush.

Drunken lawyers get drunker
and horny in boot-scoot bars.
And anyplace warmer than the river
is sanctuary for the homeless.

What makes sense holds little
meaning when you're just
damn cold, the prairie is frigid,
the horses grunt and bellow.

The Night Bus

Street corners are needful things,
where varied forms of life gather.
There's a troll walking on his hands,
and a man who waits for the light
to turn green, but never crosses to
the other side. He calls the troll

Sweetie Pie, which insults the troll.
And passersby, weighed by things
they hoped for, wait at the curb to
see, far off, the children who gather
and huddle under the streetlight,
where no one holds their hands.

There's a gnome with no hands,
lost in the mingled lineage of troll,
who hails a taxi parked by the light
of the store window, where things
for sale and things for rent gather
in lots, like things are supposed to

do. Ladies of the faith stroll by to
pass shiny tracts into the hands
of anyone who happens to gather
with the gnome and the troll,
as men who sell needless things
rest their briefcases in the light

of the oncoming bus, their plight
unknown from this point on to
the next station, while the things
they hawk rest in their hands.
"Take me with you," cries the troll,
as salesmen and hookers gather

to sort out who gets to gather
in the soft glow of moonlight.
"Sleep with us," shout the troll
and the gnome, having nothing to

do but love a woman's hands
and the other gentle things

made to gather things together,
to light their smokes, to shake
the gnarled hands of the troll.

At the Present

At the present age I think
about fog In the lowlands,
fog on the road, fog on the
dam and the river trees,

fog that ghosts the parks
and city streets to guide the
light of day through the veil.

At the present age I think
about flowers and birds.
I also wonder about dirt
for no better reason than
life is designed by the stuff.

At the present age I deny
the poet I see in mirrors,
windows, photographs.
*Surely, old boy, that's not
me,* I say to my aging self.

At the present age I'm keen
for awakening more than
sleep, and dread the long,
last nap that keeps the soul

from quandary about any
new and wondrous thing
that crawls on its belly.

Things Happen in Threes

Three days of deer, rowdy on the roads.
Three days of hope for rain in the gutters
and lawns of the neighborhood.

Three days of squirrels barking in the woods.
Three doves scratch for corn and seed.
Three days of this and that, mostly that.

Three days of Nervous Nellie down the block,
who dreads the approach of winter doldrums
that drag him face-down to the river.

2.
Three days of dearth, and plenty of it.
Three days of lint and nickels on the transom.
Three days of harvest in the heartland,

as combines coffer wheat for the masses.
Three days of moonlight, full and griseous.
Three days of homeless gnomes in the grass,

where ditch lilies stood in my neighbor's
garden, before the clotheshorse bucked her off,
and she moved to better digs.

3.
Three days with cumulonimbus clouds
that bring needed comfort to the parched
murder of crows on the levy.

Three KU girls pass by in review, like starlets
strutting their September stuff, fandangos
of blue and crimson, a wisp of rosewater.

Three dogcatchers sniff the ground
for a clue which will finally close the case
of the rabid Chihuahua.

I Have Decided

I have decided to kiss
my father's daughter.
Just a quick peck on the
lips, something I often
do when it's called for.

I have decided to hold
her as my sister, who
died before she left the
placenta, and did not
cry to the slap of life.

I have decided to buy
her clothes and burn the
dress she always wears,
the one she bought from
the Salvation Army.

I have decided not to
go with her, when she
slips the boundaries of
gravity, floats through
fields after twilight,

and pulls herself
tall in corn stubble, her
eyes scoping the ruin,
her many voices falling
on the bluestem.

Off the Beaten Path

This is not the smooth
trail, paved and straight,
the manmade footpath
you share with crowds,
no worries along the
way, safe and bored.

This path leads hard
into the wilderness.
Where you find your
way by being yourself,
outsider, one-of-a kind,
orphan of the norm.

Here you find the edge
of society's precipice,
no mirrors, standards,
or measuring sticks.
Here you take the sure
fork that leads through

woods darker than night,
fog in the trees, and the
terrible, wonderful glitter
of goblin grass, weeds
among the wallflowers
efflorescing.

II

The Night It Rained for Years

We could hear asphalt wash
from shingles through gutters
that channeled the rain to ground.
Hours passed darkly into weeks,
months, years, eons, through
burnt fields, breaking the drought.

We could feel the walls swell
with flood about to burst the house.
We wondered if nighthawks would
fall from the sky to the sewers.
We stood in the doorway and called
the moon to show itself.

Barricades at street corners
shuffled traffic past the flooded
transoms, where beer bottles
and grass wedged on the grates,
where my father's daughter
searched for her shoes.

OZ Revisited

(with apologies to L. Frank Baum)

Glinda delivers her third child,
and will not return to the stage,
now that exotic dancing no longer
pays, and horny men can see
her strip on the internet.

Munchkins, still the quaint
people, now have satellite TV,
beer and Monday Night Football.
Bored, they bounce in bed
and increase the population.

The Scarecrow finally came out,
and lives quietly with Roger
in Emerald City's East Side,
where he's loved by the locals
for giving so much poetry.

Across from the courthouse,
the statue of Toto, covered with
flying monkey shit, honors
the terrier who was mercifully
put down for complications.

The Tin Man smokes cigars
and tends bar at the Stars & Garter,
spouting homespun philosophy
to anyone who gives a damn.
And few do.

Dog Logic

Our best mutt had his own idea
of dog imagined and dog himself,
not a rocket scientist by any means,
the snuffling husky that farted.

At night he padded through the
house, took his leisure at the foot
of our bed, and chased rabbits in his
sleep, the front legs churning.

I think he sensed he had it made,
compared to pets abandoned at
the side of the road, or dropped off
at the pound without remorse.

I'm not saying he wasn't a pain in
the ass at times, like any good dog.
I'm only saying the monthly worm
pills, trips to the veterinarian, the

need to roam the neighborhood,
early morning and hourly walks,
scarfing run-over squirrels in the
street, defined the coin of dog.

And after the put-down from age,
disease and confusion, he takes
his walks through the house at
night, just to let us know how

unfair it was to hold him lovingly,
trustingly, as if we would take
him home, while the chemicals
worked their grievous chore.

Taking the Dog Out

She's up and needs to go
outside in the storm.
We're a couple of night souls.
The rain, cool and quick,
falls in the neighborhood.

She squats, pulls the leash,
strains and shakes her collar,
until it jingles like keys.
At this time of night,
no one complains

about one small dog and the shit
she leaves, me in my
nightclothes and house-shoes,
a homunculus,
awkward in the dark.

Tree in a Field

Surrounded by dandelions, flanked on
sky, the elm bends where a house stood
and left a trace of work in the grass.

I can drive past on the soft dirt road,
or stop to search for remnants of mortar,
wood and brick, or the iris gone wild,

where ghosts of memories haunt
the lespedeza, bluestem, creosote
posts and jimsonweed.

Maybe horses grazed and cantered,
showing off like they do, when humans
savor the nature of the beasts.

Perhaps a man like my grandfather,
stoic, German, stern to the bone,
walked this field with cattle and dogs.

You Might Wake Up

You might wake up in
the middle of the night
with a book on your face.
You might wake up and
find yourself alone in
the living room.

You might wake up
to a saxophone playing
in the drawer you forgot
to shut. You might wake up
with the ghost of reason
pointing an empty sleeve.

You might wake up
with no more purpose
than to climb from the
gutter to the curb,
where the night bus rushes by
in a blur of wheels.

You might, after all
wake up to find
that an angry elm is
dragging you by your
feet to the river
and the dark rapids.

You might wake up
in a strange motel
on a dead end street,
where the city devolves
to prairie that sleeps
with the corn.

Whoever You Are

The postman on the porch never rings twice.
Nor the milkman, charwoman, junkman,
baglady, the plumber or Jehovah's Witness.
Not the mailman who's also a Freemason.
Perhaps Jimmy Hoffa searches for his face,
or a snowman glitters in the morning rain.

Whoever you are, stranger, slimed with rain,
standing in the dawn's light, ringing twice:
It's time to move on with your wet, dark face,
shape-shifter in the fog, watchman, junkman,
whoever you are; father, daughter, Freemason,
hangman, Mormon, Jehovah's Witness.

There's never just one Jehovah's Witness
standing on the porch, righteous in the rain.
And I know you're not a Moose or Freemason,
the junkman, who laid the ragwoman twice,
or the daughter of the ragwoman and junkman,
the grease of labor and love on her face.

Meanwhile the dawn fog holds your face,
Mormon missionary, Jehovah's Witness,
tattered ragwoman and soused junkman,
who doesn't give a damn about the rain.
Whoever you are, stranger, I'll say it twice:
You cannot be a Moose or Freemason.

You cannot be a Moose or Freemason,
standing around with rain on your face.
The postman would never ring twice.
I know you're not a Jehovah's Witness.
And if you want to stand there in the rain,
make way for the sodden junkman.

Nobody hates the ragwoman or junkman,
more needful than the iceman or Freemason,
a clergyman who preaches to the cold rain,

the fisherman with nets billowed to the surface,
the Mormon and the Jehovah's Witness,
the hangman who never hangs anyone twice.

So go ahead and stand in the rain, junkman.
Ring twice Freemason, Jehovah's Witness.
No one will see you fall on your face.

Clearing

for Jared, one of Angelman's Angels

Out went the light in eyes that saw
what those who knew you could not take in.
You've passed through another door
and will not look back at the portal
that wedged you in darkness.

This happens to everyone, sooner
or later, who stumble, as we do, through
hundreds of rooms in a lifetime
of doorknobs and latches.

A door opens for the whiff of an instant
and closes before we take hold
of the knob, leaving us dazed with
our thumbs cocked on our temples,
shaking our heads, wondering what
went wrong in the scheme of things.

No one has ever seen death's door
and found it chained and bolted.
Even the near-death-experience
lacks the proper hasp and hinge.

And now you stand on the other side
and survey the new landscape
where fog in the meadow lifts.

Days of Work and Reason

Monday morning I wake up
and putter to the living room
to catch the early news.
Then I reckon the newscaster
has missed some local event,
so I read the newspaper.

I want to linger longer in the
house, to go out in the morning
air, see what's going on in the
neighborhood, down the block
and around the corner.

On Tuesday I wake up heavy
from the weight of reason,
and pick through the day that
follows to its logical end.

Wednesday the trash-man
comes in the dull green truck,
calling trashcans to rise on
the curb, where dogs gnash
and claw for scraps.

In the middle of the week
the world goes on with
constancy and permanence
that holds us to place.

Thursday has its own idea,
unspectacular to say the least,
ordinary, lacking validation
of how we're all flung
through the starry cluster.

And ah, Friday's a blessed girl,
who's nearly angelic in her plain
frame, who pulls me from bed
by the left foot, and laughs
at my idiosyncrasies.

For James Wright

1.
I find myself taking inventory
of a life that has not moved well
in crowds and churches.

James, I too have walked alone
on paths cut firm through farmland
and plowed woods.

With place in my blood,
I've seen the horizon of prairie,
where rails meet and roads converge.

2.
Though I've never been to Hell's Revival,
I received an invitation from
the Old Boy himself.

In fifty years a mind gets cluttered
with introspection and extrapolations
that crash the gates of sleep.

And it's no good to wear my head
like a pumpkin on a stick, a scarecrow,
brainless, full of mice.

3.
One has to traipse through life
and air the memories out like laundry.
Perhaps that is why Introverts

choose poetry for the hardtack
on which we gnash our teeth.
James, I hold you in solitude,

as I stroll the railroad tracks
and back-roads that meander
through rust.

Late in the Day

Not much happens, really.
I've sat by the window a long
time, watching the river birch
do absolutely nothing but
stand in the same old place.
The ragged peel of the bark,
no different than yesterday,
hangs loose for the show.

Thing is I rather like the tree
we planted as a sapling, thin,
delicate, apt to die at first frost.
And you'd think to look at it,
as it rose and spread the limbs,
that death was imminent.
But through the years several
branches sheltered the birds.

I gaze out the window and
ponder the next few lines.
A squirrel pads across the roof.
The roses look a bit ragged
after last night's hailstorm.
The coffee I savor will cool
in the cup, losing its charm,
and I will rise and meander

to the kitchen, pour another
cup, return to the computer,
and revise my muse to fit
the aging of the day, from
dawn crying in her diapers
to mid-afternoon, and me
wedged in this languid hour,
when words fly blind.

The Ghost of My Father's Ghost

The ghost of my father died in winter
when snow fell hard on the trees.
And as the storm spun to blizzard,
we journeyed to Nebraska,
where my father's remains were
lowered into the black earth.

Now the ghost of my father's ghost,
too much alive, owns my head
in all the mirrors of our house.
Sometimes some ghosts never die,
but haunt available planes.

It might be metaphysical, this
magic of glass, the ghost of my
father's ghost, scratching a head
grayed by degrees of guilt.
It's not so much an inheritance
as a haunting, immutable, fixed.

In this play I become my father,
dead cells sloughed with age,
the doctor that never calls,
memories lost in the lobes.

What I Know About Ghosts

Their longings are often strong
enough they sleep with the living
when revenants are scarce.

They wish to live and love again,
to repeat the same old errors,
to suffer the baser emotion

of skin love, fragile as glass.
They avoid mirrors at all costs.
And portraits of themselves,

that hang on the walls, remind them
of triumph and loss, joy and sex,
the breach of the placenta.

And I have learned from the ghosts
who loved me without reservation
that passion is best served cold

those nights when the dead
hold the living close, and love
lies bleeding in the heart.

Open Range

In the one saloon at Haigler,
a village in need of town,
the barmaid says she's new
in these parts, only lived here
five years, and has never heard
of the Arikaree Breaks.

We stroll across the street
to the general store, where local
women sell groceries and maps.
Hungry, we pay for sandwiches
made in Texas, knowing that
bread warms the belly.

On washboard roads we find
the Breaks, among beige sand hills
and cliffs gouged by the river,
where rust knits the autumn trees
with certainty of winter's approach,
and cows graze un-fenced.

One young steer stands by the
road, black against the sage.
Others chew their cuds and
drool, waiting for the farmer's
dogs to nudge them home
in the blue-gray evening.

Phew!

That smell is roadkill,
deer, skunk or raccoon,

the farm-cat or lost dog
that somebody loved.

That smell we call death's
rancor never quite leaves

the scene of the dying:
car-wreck, suicide,

homicide, heart attack,
lethal injection and war.

That smell of stale beer
at 2 a.m. floats through

bars past closing time,
the last call for alcohol,

when sensibilities blur
and brains opt out.

That smell in church,
from the next pew back,

escapes with flatulent
relief for gaseous bloat

of a colon doing triage
on last night's beans.

That smell in some houses
means that families

and their animals find
coexistence with smoke,

sweat, urine, sour milk
and responsibility.

Pondering

I step into a Christian bookstore
to buy a CD for my daughter.
And it hits me, the smell of church.
Not just bibles bound in vellum
or shiny tracts by the gross.
More than that, it's the milieu of religion,
where I pause for a moment by
posters proclaiming a local revival.

No one asks if they can help me
because I surely smell like an agnostic,
who's only here for the greatest hits
of somebody I've never heard.
I glance at the jewelry of faith:
crucifixes that dangle
from chains and lanyards.

Some have gentile Saviors
posed with the same agony.
The souvenirs of salvation are displayed:
sweatshirts, bumper-stickers, Jesus-fish,
digital portraits of the saints.
My thoughts begin to reel as the aroma
of choir loft intensifies with every
step I take past the hymnals.

And then I sweat like hell,
as I stand at the register with my
credit card, wondering if there
isn't some secret factory
that manufactures faith.

To Simply Live

Karen Carpenter, 1950 –1983

It seems that grace and talent
were not enough, nor the pure,
melancholic croon that left us
craving, calling for encores.
To simply live was insufficient.
And she is no less dead now
than Marilyn, Sylvia or Anne,
though death by their own hands
came awkward but sure,
not by degrees of vomit.
The guilt cannot ride on her
alone, but on the milieu of the
Seventies, where she was too
fat as beauty was measured
and misconstrued by the
purveyors of skin-and-bone,
who live with knowing
they sent her to the Auschwitz
of fashion, like so much
chattel.

Hoarfrost

Lovers of gooseflesh,
how happy they are

to be wrapped in wool,
jogging the dirt roads

and cold brick streets.
Some like to make snow angels

rise and serve the lord
of black ice and arctic wind.

Others remain like monks
in their houses, staring

into lapis lazuli flames
fueled by the final farts of T-Rex,

while gnarled ice trolls
have spontaneous sex

with flower fairies, homeless
in the snow, naked,

unabashed, pixilated flirts;
drunk on slush martinis.

The Year of the Gadfly

was the year that Jennie
wrote poems of hummingbirds
and leaches, butterflies
and mad cows, blue herons,
grey herons, dismal fish.

We tried to make it through
the black hole of winter,
when trees bared their knees,
and Jenny caught the hubris
that was going around.

In the rumble of April
I dragged my soul in the rain.
And the neighbors slept
like no one awkward or
sinistral lived on our block.

In the long nights of June,
I fished with Jenny Wren,
who floated like a ghost
through Constant Park's
riparian trees.

Bluestem

The year she loved me
Ed Sullivan died, and
there was no beating
around the bush, our
love was cluttered by
what might happen to
the next unlucky guy.

And while it is true
Ed Sullivan died from
a brief and private bout
with esophageal cancer,
who's to say her love for
me was not in the final
analysis to blame.

For when she loved me
The A's beat the Mets,
and she cared nothing
for baseball outside of
the sheets, where runs
were scored and tallied
in the innings of skin.

And who among us
kept record of the faith,
when love fell into
the bog of regrets?
Certainly not the prisoners
of Kansas, where only
the grass endures.

The Bishop's Wife Revisited

The bishop finally gets his cathedral,
while through the city the homeless,
hookers, agnostics, and the lost die
cold, as the spires point heavenward.

In the rectory Mildred Cassaway
makes her play for the Bishop,
who she's craved for years, and plants
smooches on his pious lips.

Sudden need for skin, they fall to the floor,
wrapped in the heat and pulse. The suit,
cross, clerical collar, all the accoutrements
of faith, flutter to the carpet.

While Julia, tired of the Ecclesial life,
the prim deportment, seduces Dudley
in the back of Sylvester's cab, and throws
caution for a lovely, magic man.

Dudley gives up power and immortality
to fuck her for a few mortal minutes;
an angel with no more purpose,
counting loss as gain in the long run.

Together they find pure joy in the park,
and make snow-angels with adulterous glee.
Julia's nipples shine in the moonlight,
as Sylvester lingers and rolls his own.

Meanwhile the camera pans the scene
of two souls finding happiness in snow.
Julia groans and bounces at the same time,
as Dudley holds her firm in the wind.

The Boy Who Kissed His Sister

The boy who kissed his sister
and the sister who didn't object,
and the dog who could care less,
the horseman stomping in his boots,
the night train drifting slowly by,
the garden gnome in the grass,
going on like nothing happened.

The garden gnome in repose,
pissing on the black-eyed daisies,
and the boy who kissed his sister,
whose pretty head reeled, until
the cows came home, as cows will
do, hoof to hoof, snorting through
the fields of windblown hay.

The night train wheeling diesel,
the cow manure in the fields,
the fairy ring and the lespedeza,
the horseman straining for truth,
beside the whitewashed porch,
and the boy who kissed his sister
pleasing himself in the privy.

And the sister, tall in her chaps,
searches for a strayed horse
in the fields of windblown hay,
the fairy ring and the lespedeza,
the cow manure in the brome,
the whippoorwill in the fescue,
and the dog gnawing its tail.

And the horse comes home in
due time, when the moonlit
fairy ring exudes with fireflies
in the field of windblown hay,
timothy, fescue and brome,
as the gnome smokes his stuff
in the black-eyed daisies.

The Fiddler

Loxosceles reclusa

You will not see him
ghost into your room,

carrying the violin
upside down on his back.

He hasn't come in darkness
to entertain you.

Matter of fact, he'd rather not.
But now that he's here,

you give him enough
space to rosin up the bow

for an arpeggio, concerto,
maybe even bluegrass.

Something by Mozart
or Wagner. A requiem

will suffice. A death mass,
hellfire and brimstone,

the fiddler knows how
to play them hot.

III

Boy

Years ago I wrote about
the girl who stood in the
snow at side of the road
and waited for the bus.

And now it's you, boy,
without your coat, like
the farm girl, who also
stood in dawn's chill,
wet-haired and dour.

Where she is now and
how she lives, with so
many years slipped past,
I haven't a blessed clue.

I only know that as I
pass, firm in the cocoon
of car, you hold your
pack and notebook.

And the bus, awkward
in what's called yellow,
that rattles adolescent
spines, will not arrive
without fanfare,

when the red lights flash
as it grunts with labor
and seepage of fumes
that fog the plains.

Rooster

> Good morning Weathercock
> How did you fare last night?
> —Ian Anderson

January

The weathervane
wails dark arias for
hoarfrost on windows,
snow on the roof,
silence like death
in the trees, a vacant
room in the house.
Arctic blasts cut
the hardened landscape.
Icicles drip from eves
and fall at night
to shatter like glass,
arousing the cattle
from their sleep.

April

Ridging the prairie
from thirty feet up,
he sings to blossoming
tulip trees, forsythia,
loosestrife and daffodils;
eager to burst forth
in motley frocks.
Spun by a zephyr
to point northward,
he watches turkey vultures
glide silent
above the plowed earth
and fields ablaze in
the burning time.

July

For brown soybeans
and worm-gnawed corn,
he cries the blues like
Coltrane's sax.
And the windsock,
hung limp for weeks,
will not stir the heat.
The weathercock
sings of burnt circles
behind the barn,
where a roman candle,
badly made and unattended,
nearly set the house on fire.

October

Now there is fog
and chill in the woods.
My father's daughter
glides through the meadow,
as the moon's trail
of shadow tricks
the dogs to howl
at blown newspapers
and tumbleweeds,
the weathercock's
rusty spin, the distant
symphony of nightjars
in the bois d' arc.

The Porpoise Drive-In Life

with apologies to Rick Warren,
author of *The Purpose-Driven Life.*

At the Porpoise Drive-In
life goes on all night.
The neon sign that says
We Never Close means
what it says: open 24/7.

Three shifts of carhops
wearing porpoise hats
deliver fast-food
on roller-skates, the resin
wheels gathering gum.

And even though the
nearest ocean is a three-day
drive, the Porpoise Drive-In
serves the best seafood
in the vast, flat land.

Past sundown the future
farmers congregate
in the parking lot, their
truck stereos blaring
Lynyrd Skynyrd,

testosterone hung
in the night air like fog,
wolf-whistles applauding
the rhythmic sway
of future farmwives.

Hay Barn

Things get hot under a tin roof.
Although I can't imagine the
round bales feel the heat like men.
Cattle tracks lead behind the
gray frame built from hedge.

Manure, the artifact of grazing
and farting, dries in the heat.
Blue flies in holding patterns
drone above the prairie grass
like planes in the distance.

Earth flattens from this point
to the vast expanse of lea,
where cocklebur will hold the fur
of a farm dog that passes close
and prods the horses home.

She Had Horses

A lovely horse of distinct breed
grazes on bluestem and lespedeza,
then turns her supple neck to look
me square in the eyes, like she knew
all along I was watching her from
my perch on the fence.

How marvelous she understands
I love a proud horse, hard to hold.
The kind no dark-cloaked specter
or headless horseman can master.
And she calls to memory the girl I
loved, who died in her 15th year.

She had horses not unlike this
yearling that strokes the ground
with her right front hoof.
For a moment I want to whisper
softly the name of Jen, shinny
the rails, hug her great neck.

But the filly somehow knows that I
will not climb the fence to stroke
her mane, coo in her ear like a lover.
I will just stand here, transfixed,
praiseful, amazed at the firm
gestalt of horse.

Nothing to Do with Horses

I think the wrens may be stalking me.
And the praying mantis in the sedum
will have my head if I falter.

Grasshoppers look particularly vicious,
the crickets have organized a band,
snails have donned their battle attire.

Nothing has anything to do with horses.

No one speaks for wind in the yews.
Two dogwoods bark at the same time,
out of synch and disharmonious.

Nobody stands in the crabgrass naked.
But that would be a nice distraction
in the current age of boredom.

The Gospel of Bubba

When Bubba took to drink and sacrificing cows,
the farmers chained and locked their barns.
Some stood outside at night, wary and armed.
Others unleashed their dogs to roam at will,
to search through bramble, howling deep,
should Bubba try to sneak through barbed wire.

When Bubba took to stealing barbed wire,
the farmers fearing the loss of their cows,
built earthworks and motes, twenty feet deep,
encircling the cattle pens, hay bales, and barns.
And all the farmers vowed to fire at will
if Bubba tried to cross, armed or unarmed.

When Bubba took to riding the range, armed
with tin-snips to cut through barbed wire,
wearing only bobby socks, knit in twill,
he searched by starlight for wayward cows;
chewing their cuds, straying from the barns,
mewling by the motes, dank and deep.

When Bubba took to scuba diving the deep
motes by night, half-crazed and armed,
the farmers laid minefields by the barns,
behind tall fences of concertina wire.
So much depended on the gentle cows,
and Bubba was drunk with fierce will.

When Bubba took to guzzling rot-gut swill,
and drove his Hummer on the banks of deep
streams, constantly searching for cows,
all the farmers stayed vigilant and armed,
behind the earthworks and razor wire;
like minutemen, guarding their barns.

When Bubba found religion for red barns,
prayed, fasted and surrendered free will,
he flung himself on the concertina wire,

hanging naked as the blood ran deep.
The farmers gathered, awed and armed,
as steers grazed with the cows.

And the wire still hangs by the barns,
where cows graze unharmed, with bovine
brains that lack free will or deep thought.

She Sings Pink Floyd

All too well she knows
the dark depth of their
lyrics, the melancholy
prose, the rhymed and
versed biographies.

She longs for validation
whenever she can find it,
which is difficult for
my father's daughter,
who rises at midnight

and floats around town,
singing *Hey You, Us and
Them, Wish You Were
Here,* and *Shine On
You Crazy Diamond.*

Once in a Meadow

Once in a meadow I saw you
walking on your hands, somersaulting,
turning cartwheels in the brome.
You were on the other side of the road.
I was behind the old red barn.
A shrew pissed in the manure.
Crows stripped the fallen corn.

Once in a blue moon I see you
standing silent in the hedgerow.
And every once in a while you
pull yourself together enough
to drive around on the back-roads,
stirring the dust, swerving with
purpose, plowing the trees.

Every now and then you see me
standing with my hands in my pockets,
thumbs cocked like James Dean,
watching you feed the ducks.
Casting bread on the water,
your saintly delusion counts
for nothing in the avian world.

Tonight in a pasture I see you
riding the tall white horse,
bathed in the light of a gibbous moon,
wearing nothing but boots and the hat
you bought at the five & dime.
Nothing you do, somnambulist,
can measure up to that.

Horsefeathers

Someone's laughing, Lord, kumbaya
Someone's laughing, Lord, kumbaya
Someone's laughing, Lord, kumbaya
O Lord, kumbaya
      —traditional folk song

Yesterday a dogwood howled and I didn't care.
The mail was late. The garbage stunk.
There was nothing on TV but reruns of Sarah Palin.

I've read every book in the house worth
reading, replayed everything I forgot
about faith, sat in the dark like a monk.

My soul looks familiar, but I can't
quite place where I've seen it before.
Nobody's here. God's on vacation.

The town lies knitted in dark wool.
Cars roar up and down the street,
leaving exhaust clouds, thick as fog.

And all creatures that live in fog,
vampires, werewolves and terrorists,
have taken the night bus to hell,

where at least it's warm enough
to gather by the eternal bonfire
and burst into song.

Bonfire of the Sleepless Poet

I can't ash my brain down
or quell the flame of thought
and verse milling around.
I mull about trivial things.
I tried the cognitive method
of stopping thoughts.
I bought the cassette tapes
with sleep inducing sounds
like loons gliding on the lake
and jungle rain with birdcalls.
Past midnight I opened
the bedroom window and
listened to the night opera's
chorus of moonglow and the
questions posed by ordinary air.
I have wasted time pondering
the brevity of life, longing
to age slowly and not burn-out
like driftwood up in smoke.

In Case of Aging

I can tell you that my first grade
teacher's name was Clara Bell.
She kept a brass bell on her desk,
and a set of Dutch Boy nesting dolls.

You cannot say that I misremember.
Or in case of aging I forget the details
of my life as they occurred, with no
confabulation of the aging brain.

I can tell you that I masturbated like
every other boy, loving by proxy the
girls of my time and place, moaning
with joy, learning blessed things.

In case of aging I forget to mention
that I once held onto Dean,
as we danced to *Unchained Melody*,
palms wedged, never stumbling.

Bird Flu Gloves

I gather fresh-cut grass in March,
as slow wind lifts the tasseled heads
enough to uncover one dead bird,

a robin, common to Kansas as crow.
How it died is anyone's guess,
but the neighbor's parakeet was not involved.

And no self-respecting stray cat
would kill a robin and leave it as it lies,
head attached, wings unruffled.

Lifting it gently with covered
hands, and holding my breath,
I drop it into the trash.

The Night We Heard the Whippoorwill

The night we heard the whippoorwill,
we sat on rocks in Constant Park,
our hair mussed from the wind.
The florets of love-lies bleeding
held red in spite of the darkness.
We watched Cassiopeia and Orion
slow-dance to moon music.

Blowing the sure laws of physics,
clouds rolled behind the moon.
You slugged me and spoke of horses,
horseflies, horse-sense, how they
converge in the plausible world.
Fireflies looped above the grass.
Fog ghosted through the trees.

The night we heard the whippoorwill
was not the last night of our lives.
That night came in winter,
when the nightjar's song was silent,
and the dirge of dead oaks
drove us to the high loess
cliffs above the river.

Awakened by Silence

If winter has aroused me,
I am of all men most disturbed
by the mute snowfall.
There must be quiet tumults
in silence so deafening it splits
the lobes of an aging brain.

I sit up in bed and look around
to find no color on my retinas,
only the dumb shades of gray,
air so laconic it ghosts the room,
and the muted cry of a lost poem,
wedged in the reticent void.

If the snow speaks of nothing
worth knowing, and drifts
by the curb stay mum, all that's
clear in this time and place
is that one noise, faint or taciturn,
will scream like a riot in the walls.

Shades of Gray

To the men who shot the whooping cranes

You thought they were
common sand hill cranes
that wade the prairie shores,
tall, gray birds that will not
stand regaled in white
with black-tipped wings.

An accident is your plea.
Shades of gray blinded you
with the need to blast any bird
rising in that vague instant
when trigger-fingers
twitch and barrels roar.

Mistaken identity stands
as your claim of shame.
Any real hunter knows the target
and reason to kill, shrouded
as it is in right-or-wrong,
morality and hubris.

Blinded by testosterone,
your retinas blended
white to gray.
In this there is no living color,
only the shades of
passenger pigeons.

The Ivory-billed Woodpecker

Listed as perhaps extinct

The last one seen and verified
was shot, stuffed and displayed
for no more reason than
because no law was passed
to stem the slaughter.

The things we do astound me,
shooting the wild and lovely
thing, because no one was there
to slap the hands, say no-no.

Because no law was passed,
no barter made, no rule applied,
we cut the clear path for extinction.

Nothing was done by anyone
for birds more wronged than eagles,
more scare than whooping cranes,
listed as endangered, but seen
and verified.

The hue and cry of men with
guns and nothing better to do
does so much damage to the
natural order of things.

And for no more reason
than because no law was passed,
a species slips to the shadow
of doubt, maybe gone, maybe
not, no way to be sure.

The View from Sanders Mound

From here the way goes soft for geese.
And across the lake, barely visible,
a sailboat rides the waves toward shore.

I think of the walrus and the carpenter,
who walked along a sandy beach,
not unlike the one below.

They wept for oysters in their bellies,
because they had deceived them
and eaten them all.

But one has to dig for days here,
to find a mollusk worth the effort,
and even then toss it back.

Pelicans look like swans to two men
who hug and kiss on the riprap.

Elders, they seem to blend together
like the long married; and in this milieu
no one cares about who loves who.

Driftwood tangled along the sandbar
holds the moss and debris like lattice.

Beer cans and green bottles glint.
Cars rush by on the dam. Girls on
bicycles rest at the spillway.

Vultures in a Dead Tree

At Clinton Lake I sit
in the heat and watch
them watching me
with needless trepidation.
I am more wary of them
then they are of me.

And every now and then
one of them glides from
a branch, circles above
me, drops to the ground,
and stares at bloated
carp in the distance.

A solution to the problem
is obvious in bird logic:
the lack of opposable thumbs
will not prevent them
from waiting for the lake
to give-up her dead.

Stranger at the Door

You want to get that, hon?
I'm really busy at the moment,
watching the robber fly
that's perched on our window
and might try to rob us.
And besides I haven't a thing to wear.

You want to get that, hon?
I can see from where I stand,
watching a dragonfly
preen its mandibles,
that the man totes a briefcase
full of Watchtower magazines.

And besides I haven't a thing to wear.
And the stranger stands at the door
watching black flies
size him up for a bite.
I'm really busy at the moment,
drinking wine and cutting cheese.

You want to get that, hon?
Or would you rather stand there,
watching a deerfly
collide with the screen,
as you knit a turtleneck sweater
and the stranger stands at the door?

I can see from where I stand
the stranger at the door,
watching horseflies encircle
his head, slapping at the buzz,
flailing like a windmill
in rough weather.

Curtain Call

The tattooed weightlifter,
whose face would wreck
a battleship, whose head is shaved,
who rolls her own cigarettes
and lights her lover's libido,
teaches advanced piano
and interpretive dance.

Rubber Girl and the Horse-
faced Boy, who raised three
children that call themselves
blessed, live for the grandkids
scattered across the land.
She's head of the knitting guild.
He's volunteer fire-chief.

Snakeman still does shows
at malls and county fairs,
where he crawls on his belly
with the rattlesnakes,
cobras, and black mambas.
Bitten twenty-five times,
he's immune to the venom.

Queen Natasha has retired
to the nudist farm, and no one
carries on the old illusion.
But through it all she's kept
the gorilla suit and bikini,
knowing that even now
there's hope for an encore.

While She Sleeps

While she sleeps oblivious to the
noise, I rise to search the house,
knowing all the ghosts have flown
north in search of cooler haunts.
The yard light bends its lumens
through the living room window,
so that I might know the path.

Difficult as it is without glasses,
I stand at the front door and find
the lock and deadbolt secure.
And that's as it should be in the
house at night, where even the
darkness shines a pure shaft,
as angels wrestle with doubt.

I have seen a few of the angels
tiptoe naked around the house,
leaving their clawed footprints
in the hallway, and their castoff
robes in the clothes hamper.
But in times like these, when
the noise awakens me, they

can't be found to save my soul.
So here I stand befuddled,
gazing out the backdoor at 2 am,
seeing nothing but the vague
glow of moon through clouds,
something moving in the grass,
the furtive drift of raccoon.

Bile Diary

As human pincushion I'm poor fare,
my chest strung to this beeping box,
my right arm firm to the saline drip.
And lord love a duck, I cannot move
more than enough to stand, hoist
this flimsy gown and piss in a jug.

Hospitals are strange motels, all
the pictures on the walls even worse
than some sleazy pay-by-the-hour
flophouse, where the rendezvous
of passion is dark and desperate.
There's a nurse I could love in some

other life, minus thirty-five years.
She wants to help me trundle to the
bathroom, dragging the goddamned
apparatus that announces, digitally,
that my pulse is viable, the blood
pressure's fine, etcetera, etcetera...

I could love her in that parallel place,
If not for the love of my wife, if not
for the fact that I am that kind of dull,
drab bard who cannot allow himself
the joy of loving two women at once.
Lord love a duck, call me a pilgrim.

And now it comes to the surgery,
when the gallbladder is expendable,
a vestigial thing that complicates my
life, not unlike the adenoids or the
tonsils I surrendered to the scalpel
at an early age, when the world

was new and the laws of life were
inchoate. I muse about this intern,
who awakens me at 2 am to hang
yet another saline bag, who softly
apologizes for disturbing my sleep,
whose nose ring flashes silver.

Vespers

Let every bug of derision,
cicada, cricket, katydid,
black fly, gnat and no-see-um,
return with insipid drone.

Let the weeds in vacant lots
bloom in motley clumps.

Let the turkey vulture
preen its wings on burr-oaks
by the side of the road.

Let green be intensely green,
the sun do its ageless scorch,
and clothing grace nothing more
than the law requires.

Let the clarity of evening
and burnt-ends of day
hold the scent of charcoal,
beer, sweat and place.

Let night herons praise
the dark water.

Acknowledgments

Many thanks to the editors of the following periodicals, where these poems first appeared, some in slightly different forms:

Chiron Review: "Bird-flu Gloves" "Nothing To Do With Horses"
"The Gospel of Bubba"
Coal City Review: "Stranger at the Door" "Things Happen in Threes" "To Simply Live"
Flint Hills Review: "Horsefeathers" "You Might Wake Up"
Haight Ashbury Literary Journal: "Bonfire of the Sleepless Poet" "Ghost Town"
Kansas City Star: "Girl"
Kansas City Voices: "Incident at Rider's Ford" "Off the Beaten Path" "The Fiddler"
Little Balkans Review: "Taking the Dog Out"
Mad Poet's Review: "Nocturne for Mrs. McMahon"
Main Street Rag: "Hoarfrost" "My Father's Daughter"
Mother Earth International Journal: "Shades of Gray"
Mudfish: "I Saw You at the Bait Shop"
New Mexico Poetry Review: "The Water Is Smoky with Mud"
Pegasus: "Phew!" "Sunday Morning"
Pulsar Poetry Magazine (UK): "Vultures in a Dead Tree"
Rattle: "The Wind Dancing Across the Prairie"
Straylight: "Meanwhile"
Tears in the Fence (UK): "Once in a Meadow"
The Same: "Curtain Call" "The Porpoise Drive-In Life"
Thorny Locust: "Whoever You Are"
Wisconsin Review: "Year of the Gadfly" "Vespers"

"For James Wright" and "Shades of Gray" were published in *Tallgrass Voices, Poems from members of the Kansas Authors Club*: Hillsong Press, 2011.

"The Night We Heard the Whippoorwill" and "Oz Revisited" were published in *Begin Again: 150 Poems/* Edited by Caryn Mirriam-Goldberg: Woodley Memorial Press, 2011

"Late in the Day" and "Camping in the Stull Cemetery" were published in *The Whirlybird Anthology of Kansas City Writers*/Edited by Vernon Rowe, Maryfrances Wagner, David Ray, Judy Ray: Whirlybird Press, 2012.

"Ghost Town" will appear in *In the BLACK/ In the RED: Poems of Profit & Loss/* Edited by Gloria Vando & Philip Miller: Helicon Nine (not yet printed)

Gary Lechliter's poetry has recently appeared in *Main Street Rag*, *New Mexico Poetry Review*, *Straylight*, *Tears in the Fence*, *Wisconsin Review*, *Begin Again: 150 Kansas Poems,* and *The Whirlybird Anthology of Kansas City Writers*. He has published 2 books of poetry and is managing editor of I-70 Review.

The Great Poet

While I never read his work
in high school, half of my
girlfriends, which totaled one,
read to me from his books.

She said his words were deep
with warm and orange.
She said he really knew the
color wheel of the heart.

But when did we learn in the
decade of popular kitsch
that what prevailed in his poetry
was the sum of all treacle?

How did we come to imagine
a gull, a clutch of periwinkles,
your grandma's blouse that
embraced you with lint?

Looking back it seems clear
we surely must have sought
the vapid, quick and dull,
the verse so generic,

choked with ideas of the
thing, that we forgot about
the Republican Convention,
riots, Manson, the war.

www.ingramcontent.com/pod-product-compliance
Lightning Source LLC
Chambersburg PA
CBHW031204090426
42736CB00009B/781